J. WESTON
WALCH
PUBLISHER
Portland, Maine

Content-Area Writing Strategies

Language Arts

Mary Rich

User's Guide
to
Walch Reproducible Books

Purchasers of this book are granted the right to reproduce all pages.

This permission is limited to a single teacher, for classroom use only.

Any questions regarding this policy or requests to purchase further reproduction rights should be addressed to

Permissions Editor
J. Weston Walch, Publisher
321 Valley Street • P.O. Box 658
Portland, Maine 04104-0658

1   2   3   4   5   6   7   8   9   10

ISBN 0-8251-4576-7

Copyright © 2003
J. Weston Walch, Publisher
P. O. Box 658 • Portland, Maine 04104-0658
walch.com

Printed in the United States of America

Contents

.

INTRODUCTION

The *Content-Area Writing Strategies* books teach students to write essays for classroom assignments. The writing process is reviewed, and models show good writing in action.

Students move from reading about writing, through observing good writing, to creating their own solid written pieces. They learn to recognize common language arts writing patterns and employ them themselves to write effective essays. These patterns are main idea and details, opinion and supporting evidence, compare and contrast, cause and effect, and chronological order.

Graphic organizers help students generate and clarify their thoughts during the prewriting and writing stages of the writing process. These graphic organizers are embedded in the instructional pages; blanks are also found in Part 4 of this book. A revising checklist and a peer-editing form aid in the revision stage, and a proofreading checklist reminds students of the mechanics of strong writing. A grading rubric simplifies the teacher's task of scoring!

Classroom Management

Content-Area Writing Strategies is easy to use. Each lesson is a self-contained study of a part of the writing process. Simply photocopy the lesson and distribute it. You may want to model some of the Try It sections on the board or on a transparency if students need a little more help identifying the elements being discussed in a particular lesson. Lessons build on earlier lessons, so it is suggested that the lessons be explored in order.

Part 1: Prewriting

Part 1 of this book concentrates on prewriting, guiding students through the steps that lead up to writing: brainstorming, narrowing a topic, clarifying purpose, and identifying an audience. This section emphasizes the importance (necessity!) of planning in creating a worthwhile and successful final product.

Part 2: Writing Strategies

This section deals with writing strategies, giving students abundant opportunities to see good writing and then to try it themselves. It also offers useful graphic organizers to help students generate a blueprint of their piece before it is written. This helps students clarify and organize their ideas and keeps them on track while they are writing.

Part 3: Practice Readings

Part 3 of *Content-Area Writing Strategies* provides longer practice readings. You may wish to assign one of the suggested essay questions listed in the Teaching Tips section at the end of this book, to have students choose a question from the list, or to encourage students to generate their own thesis statements based on the reading.

Part 4: Graphic Organizers

This section contains blank graphic organizers for use with any writing assignment. A revising checklist, a peer-editing form, and a proofreading checklist are also included in this section.

Part 5: Teacher's Guide

The Teaching Tips and Answer Key provide ideas for each lesson, with answers for those exercises requiring them. This is also where you will find suggestions for essay questions for the practice readings (found in Part 3 of the instruction). The assessment rubric simplifies the task of scoring. You may want to customize the rubric by adding categories to the "Other" section, by adjusting point values, or by modifying the "Criteria."

The reading-writing connection is a strong one; practicing and strengthening one improves the other. *Content-Area Reading Strategies* is a companion series to this one, focusing on reading comprehension in the disciplines of language arts, social studies, science, and mathematics. The *Content-Area Vocabulary Strategies* series concentrates on using context clues and other strategies to decipher unfamiliar vocabulary in content-area reading.

PART 1
Prewriting

LESSON 1
Writing Process Review

Writing: A Skill and a Process

A *skill* is the ability to use your knowledge to do something well. Writing is a skill you learn, like reading, or jumping rope, or playing a video game. Like these other skills, writing well takes practice. You need to do it often.

Writing is also a process. A *process* is a series of actions that leads to a goal. Besides writing, what other things do you do that follow a process? List them here.

_____

_____

_____

Describe a time when you followed the steps in a process to reach a goal.

_____

_____

_____

Steps in the Writing Process

You do not sit down and write a whole essay in ten minutes. If you did, it probably would not be very good. To write a good essay, follow the steps of the writing process:

Step 1: Prewriting	Prewriting involves planning, researching, and making decisions about your writing.
Step 2: Drafting	Drafting is the actual writing of the essay.
Step 3: Revising	Revising means rereading your essay and improving it.
Step 4: Publishing	Publishing means putting your essay into its final form to share with others.

In this book, you will work on each of these four steps.

Writing Process Review *(continued)*

Prewriting   In the next four lessons, you will learn about and practice the first step, prewriting. This step can be broken down into these smaller steps:

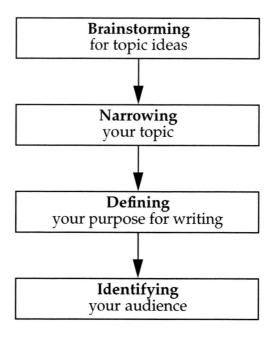

LESSON 2
Brainstorming

Brainstorming   Brainstorming means letting your mind run with an idea. Have you ever played the free-association game? In this game, a partner says a word. Then you say the first thing that pops into your mind. You don't worry about what you are going to say. You don't try to say the "right" thing. You just say whatever comes into your mind.

Brainstorming for writing ideas is like that game. Instead of saying one word, you write as many ideas as you can.

Brainstorming   One way to brainstorm is to use a web. You brainstorm ideas and write
Web   them in circles. As one idea leads to another, you join circles with connecting lines. A web helps you see your ideas and how they are related.

Let's see what brainstorming looks like. Imagine that you have to write an essay about your favorite book. Let's say that your favorite book of all time is *Charlotte's Web.* A brainstorming web might look something like this.

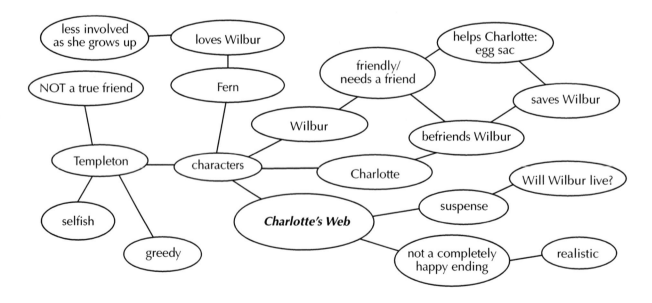

Brainstorming *(continued)*

Try It   Now try some brainstorming. Imagine that you are going to write an essay explaining why a particular book is your favorite. To jump-start your ideas, you may want to ask yourself some questions. You might ask, "Why do I like this book?" "What makes this book different from others?" "What makes me remember this book?" Questions such as these can get your ideas flowing.

Now, use the web that follows to brainstorm ideas about your favorite book. This web is just an example. You will probably want to add more circles and lines in some places and leave others out. The web is a tool for you to use. Use it in the way that works best for you.

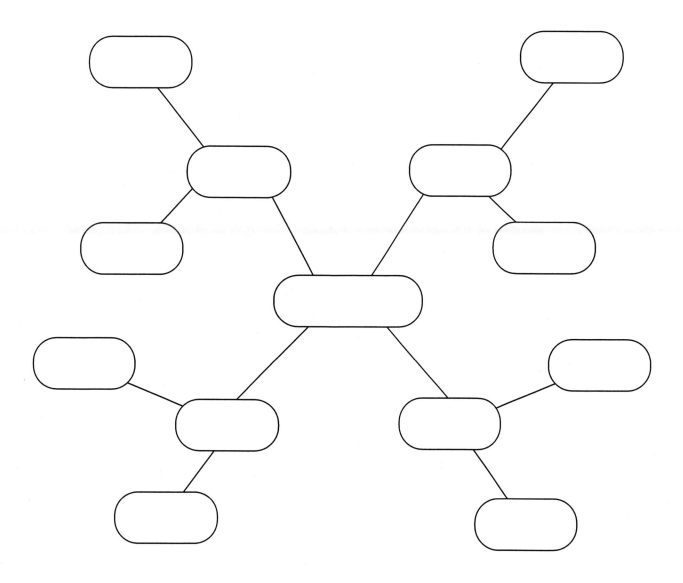

LESSON 3
Narrowing Your Topic

From Broad to Narrow

Sometimes broad is good. You want a road to be broad enough for cars to drive. When writing an essay, however, narrow is better. Narrowing your topic means breaking down your broad, or general, topic into a smaller, narrower one. A narrow topic is one that can be covered in one essay.

Use Your Web

Look at your brainstorming web on page 5. Do you see any patterns? For example, is there one area of the web that has more circles and lines? Is there one area that made you think of more questions? Is there one area—or even one circle—that really interests you? Analyzing, or looking at the parts of, your web can help you see a narrow topic within the broad one.

Imagine that you can read the mind of the person who filled in the brainstorming web about *Charlotte's Web*. When she analyzes her web, her conversation with herself might go something like this:

> Hmm. The sections about Fern and Templeton didn't go too far. I really liked the way Charlotte became Wilbur's friend when he asked for one. And it was cool the way every year some of the new spiders stayed to be Wilbur's friends. I liked the illustrations in the book, too. And the humor. But I think what I liked most about the book is what it shows about true friends.

Analyzing the web has led to a narrow topic: The theme of friendship is what makes *Charlotte's Web* the author's favorite book. The essay would go on to show the friendships in the book and tell why the essay writer likes the message behind them. This is a manageable topic that can be covered in one essay. The broad topic "my favorite book" could lead to a paper that goes on and on, talking about many interesting parts of *Charlotte's Web*. Narrowing the topic allows you to focus on one point.

Try It

Now look at the brainstorming web you filled in. Analyze the web for patterns. Based on your analysis, write a possible narrowed topic here.

_____

ESSON 4
Purpose

Why?   Why are you writing this essay? Of course, your teacher told you to. Beyond that, though, why are you writing this particular essay?

All writers write for a reason. Sometimes a writer wants to give information. Writers of computer manuals, for example, would fall into this category. People who review movies, restaurants, and books write to give an opinion. Teachers write comments on report cards to explain grades and progress. As you can see, there are many reasons to write!

As a student, you are often asked to write. A teacher—or a printed question on a test—will give a general purpose for an essay. It will still be up to you to decide how to tackle the assignment. You will have to put that plan into your own words.

State Your Purpose   Early on in any essay, you will have to state your purpose. That is, you will have to tell what you plan to show in your written piece. This statement of purpose is called a **thesis statement.** Your thesis statement is one sentence that says what you are going to tell about your topic.

Think about the "favorite book" assignment we've been practicing. The author analyzed the brainstorming web. She decided that she was really drawn to the relationship between Wilbur and Charlotte. The essay writer decided to tell why she thought this relationship was true friendship. She turned that decision into a statement of purpose: *My favorite book is* Charlotte's Web, *because it shows what true friendship means.*

Try It   Now try writing your own thesis statement. Think about your narrowed topic. Decide what you want to say about it. Write one sentence that tells what you plan to show in your essay.

_____

_____

LESSON 5
Audience

Who?

Any communication is meant for an audience. This includes novels, memos, receipts, prescriptions, speeches, reports—the list is endless.

You affect your audience by writing something that will capture their interest. Your audience affects you, too. It affects your choice of words, the length of your sentences, and the details you use.

The Effects of an Audience

Imagine writing an essay about sea animals to share with your science class. You could assume that they have the same knowledge and vocabulary that you do. What if you went to a summer camp at an ocean lab? Now you would be writing to share ideas with the scientists there. Would you use the same terms that you would with your classmates? Probably not. What if you wanted to tell a kindergarten class about the sea animals? How would a kindergarten audience affect your writing?

_____

_____

Good Writing Tip: Use Standard English

When you are writing formally, you should use Standard English. In personal notes and e-mails to friends, you may use casual language. In all other situations, you should avoid slang words, slang spelling, and poor grammar.

Thinking About the Audience

Think about the *Charlotte's Web* essay. Who is the audience? They are the teacher, maybe classmates, and people who read the student's portfolio. In this case, the language would be Standard English. The teacher and most of the other audience members will know the book. The topic of the essay is friendship and the essay writer's feelings about it. This does not call for difficult vocabulary. The discussion will be relatively simple, using examples from the book and describing the writer's feelings. These are things other people can understand.

Audience *(continued)*

Think About Your Audience

Think about the essay on your favorite book.

1. Imagine that this essay is going to be entered in a contest. The prize is a book of your choice every month for a year. The judges are editors for a big publishing company. How would this audience affect your writing?

_____

_____

_____

2. Imagine that you want to convince a younger class to read your favorite book. How would you change your writing for that audience?

_____

_____

_____

3. Imagine that you are not writing an essay but are recommending the book to a friend in an e-mail. Write that e-mail message below.

_____

_____

_____

_____

PART 2
Writing
Strategies

LESSON 6
Drafting

Drafting

Drafting means "writing." The drafting step is the point in the writing process when you actually write your essay. Drafting is not done just once but several times. Each new draft improves the one before it.

You want your finished essay to be great. One way to succeed is to put your best effort into each draft. That way you will not have to repeat the drafting step too many times.

The Parts of an Essay

When you write a first draft, keep in mind the three parts of an essay. These are the introductory paragraph, at least three body paragraphs, and the concluding paragraph.

As the name suggests, the introductory paragraph introduces the essay. This is where you put your thesis statement. The body paragraphs give information that supports the thesis statement. The concluding paragraph ends the essay. It usually restates the thesis statement in different words.

Common Patterns in Language Arts

All writing is language arts writing because it involves language. There are some patterns, though, that you are especially likely to use for language arts classes. You will see and practice each of these patterns in the coming lessons:

- Main idea and details
- Opinion and supporting evidence
- Compare and contrast
- Cause and effect
- Chronological order

Drafting *(continued)*

Are you familiar with any of these patterns? Describe when you have read or written something that follows any of the patterns.

_____

_____

_____

_____

What types of writing do you do for language arts class? Do you purposely use a pattern in your written assignments? Explain.

_____

_____

_____

_____

_____

LESSON 7
Main Idea and Details

Main idea and details is a writing pattern you will often see. In this type of organization, the main idea, or thesis, usually comes in the first paragraph. It tells you what the point of the essay is. Then details that support or prove the main idea follow in the body of the essay. The details reveal the *who*, *what*, *when*, *where*, and *why* behind the main idea.

Main Idea Versus Details

One way to decide if a sentence is a main idea sentence is to ask yourself "Is this what the essay is about?" You may need to read a bit of the essay before you can tell which sentences give main ideas and which contain details. Ask yourself "Does this give information about something else?" This will help you find the details.

These questions work whether you are dealing with a whole essay or a single paragraph.

Model

Read the following paragraph. See if you can find the main idea and details.

> The duck-billed platypus is an unusual mammal. Unlike most other mammals, it lays eggs. It also has a bill, which you expect to see on a bird. The male duck-billed platypus has a venomous spur on each hind leg. There are only two other venomous mammals. The duck-billed platypus is so unusual that it is in a scientific family of its own.

The main idea of this paragraph is the first sentence: "The duck-billed platypus is an unusual mammal." Each sentence that follows gives some information that tells how the duck-billed platypus is unusual. These are the details. The last sentence restates the main idea that this is an unusual animal.

Main Idea and Details *(continued)*

Try It Read the following passage. This essay follows the main idea-and-details pattern. See if you can find the main idea of the passage and the details that support it.

Ray Hicks was a master story-teller. He kept alive an old Appalachian oral tradition. Ray Hicks was best known for telling Jack tales. These are stories like the familiar "Jack and the Beanstalk." In them, a plucky young boy named Jack uses his wits (and luck) to overcome difficulties. Mr. Hicks also told cantefables. These are stories with songs and music added.

Mainstream media outlets were interested in Ray Hicks and his stories. He appeared in the PBS series *The Story of English.* He was asked to appear on *The Tonight Show* and *Today.* He declined both offers. He did, however, allow scholars, journalists, and others to come to his mountain to hear his stories.

Fame and acclaim were no strangers to Ray Hicks. Some-times known as "The Voice of Appalachia," Mr. Hicks was a regular headliner at the annual National Story-Telling Festival. In 1983, he received an award from the National Endowment for the Arts. He was also honored as a National Heritage Fellow.

Ray Hicks did not just tell stories; he lived them. Some of his stories were based on his own experiences. Some he learned from his grandfather, who learned them from his grand-father. Ray Hicks knew firsthand the poverty of Jack, who had to work hard just to survive. Story-telling was part of Ray Hicks's daily life.

When he died in 2003 at the age of eighty, Mr. Hicks was well-known as one of the last and best in his field. His stories have been collected in books and on audio and video recordings. The centuries-old stories Ray Hicks told will continue to be heard in his voice.

Main Idea and Details (continued)

Did you find the main ideas and details? Write **MI** on the line before the main ideas below. Write **D** before the details.

1. _____ Ray Hicks was best known for telling Jack tales.

2. _____ Ray Hicks was a master storyteller in the Appalachian tradition.

3. _____ Ray Hicks was poor, like Jack.

4. _____ The media were interested in Ray Hicks and his stories.

5. _____ Ray Hicks received an award from the National Endowment for the Arts.

6. _____ Ray Hicks lived in Appalachia.

7. _____ Many of Hicks's stories have been collected and recorded.

8. _____ Ray Hicks appeared at the National Story-Telling Festival.

9. _____ Ray Hicks told cantefables.

10. _____ When he died, Ray Hicks was known as one of the last and best in his field.

Good Writing Tip: Write a Clear Thesis Statement

To make your essay clear, you need to make your main idea clear. Do not confuse your reader with extra details or too many important ideas. State your main idea—your purpose—early in your essay.

Good Writing Tip: Use Smooth Transitions

A transition is a change from one thing to another. In writing, transitions are words that smooth the connections between ideas. They link the ideas in some way. Here are some useful transition words for main-idea-and-details essays.

To show how ideas are alike
as, also, just as, like, likewise, in the same way, similarly

To add more information
additionally, in addition, along with, also, as well as, another, besides

To conclude
as has been shown, as the evidence shows, as you can see, in conclusion, therefore

Main Idea and Details *(continued)*

Application   Now you are ready to try a main-idea-and-details essay. Read the three topics below. Then read the selections on pages 17 to 19. After reading, choose one of the topics. Write a main-idea-and-details essay based on the topic. Remember to follow the steps of the writing process.

Topics

1. Family is important in the success of young athletes.
2. Safety is an important issue in extreme sports.
3. To be successful, young champions need to start very young.

The Enders Sisters

Two of today's best—and youngest—race-car drivers in the country are young women. They're sisters, too: Erica and Courtney Enders. This pair proves that women can be successful in this highly competitive sport.

Erica Enders entered her first National Hot Rod Association (NHRA) drag race when she was just nine years old. She won that Division 4 Junior Dragster Championship, and she hasn't stopped racing since. Among her many achievements, she was named the NHRA Rookie of the Year and National Dragster's Sportsman Rookie of the Year for 2000. In 2001, she was the NHRA 50th Anniversary Race Super Pro Rail Champion. In 2002, she was the Quick 32 Number 1 Qualifier.

Courtney Enders, younger than her sister by three years, was eight years old when she began her racing career. She was the youngest fully sponsored member of the Team Pennzoil National Team. Her racing wins include three Spring Nationals Championships, a Super Chevy Show Championship, and a Division 4 Event Championship.

The Enders sisters have been around their sport since they were born; their father is professional drag racer Gregg Enders. When Erica read a magazine article about junior racing, she asked her father if she could try it. He thought it was a great idea. The girls' mother, Janet, was less enthusiastic. Erica emphasizes that drivers wear serious protective gear when they are racing. She has been injured in other sports but has never been hurt racing. Gregg Enders claims to feel safer putting his daughters into a race car than sending them off on a date.   *(continued)*

Main Idea and Details *(continued)*

The Enders Sisters **(continued)**

Although she has felt discriminated against as a girl, Erica has won over the fans. She and Courtney have also won sponsors. Having a sponsor demands success on the track and professionalism off it. They make appearances at various events for their sponsors.

Besides competing with men, the sisters compete with each other on the track and at home.

The Disney movie *Right on Track* focuses on the sibling rivalry between these two champions. Erica, a college student, plans to one day manage Enders Racing while continuing to race. Whatever their futures in racing, the Enders sisters have proved that they are female forces to be reckoned with in a male-dominated sport.

Motocross Phenom

James Stewart, Jr., is a remarkable young man in many ways. He is the youngest 125cc American Motocross Association National Champion in history. He is the first African American AMA Champion. He is also a poised, grounded teenager, despite the hype that surrounds him.

James Stewart began racing when he was four years old. His father, James Sr., had raced locally when he was younger and shared his interest with his son. James Sr. built two motocross tracks on the family's farm in Florida. James's younger brother, Malcolm, has also taken up the sport.

As soon as he was old enough, James Jr. became a professional. In 2002, he won the AMA National Championship, racked up the most wins in 125cc AMA motocross history, and had the best rookie season in motocross history. He races for Kawasaki as a professional, as he did as an amateur.

In 2002, James Stewart also became the first African American AMA champion. Eddie Graveline, sports writer and photographer, asked James Stewart in an interview if he felt added responsibility because of this fact. James replied that "we all look the same under a helmet."

James is a professional, mentioning his sponsors whenever it is appropriate. He appears comfortable with the media and the fans who now follow him. He has been compared to Tiger Woods and Jackie Robinson. James Sr. said in *Sports Illustrated Adventure*, "We don't listen to the hype."

(continued)

Main Idea and Details *(continued)*

Motocross Phenom (continued)

Like other kids, James says "cool" and "awesome" a lot. He wore braces until recently. He has been schooled at home and rides on his own race tracks often. James is also a loyal friend. He wears the racing number 259 in honor of his friend Tony Haines. Haines, who was paralyzed in a motocross accident, raced with that number. James Stewart seems to be a normal teen who has an extraordinary talent.

At the Rodeo and on the Runway

Fallon Taylor has two jobs, and she excels at both. She is a champion in barrel racing, a rodeo event. She is also a fashion model.

Fallon explains that her two professions have some similarities. They are both fast-paced, and they both give her an "adrenaline rush."

Fallon became a professional barrel racer at the age of seven. She set an arena record at the Tucson Rodeo Grounds when she was thirteen. She won the barrel-racing event again when she was nineteen.

Although barrel racing is among the safest of the rodeo events, there is still some risk of a mishap. Fallon's modeling agency has suggested that she wear a helmet when she competes.

Fallon, now a college student, rodeoed a bit while in school, but it was not her focus. She has decided to take some time off from school to get back in the saddle. She hopes to become competitive again in the ring, while keeping her poise on the runway.

Main Idea and Details *(continued)*

Prewriting **Brainstorming**

Brainstorm about the topic you choose. Change the web as needed.

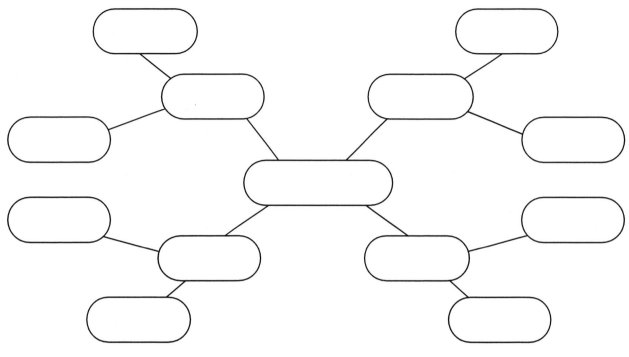

Narrow your Topic

Now analyze your web. Then write your narrowed topic.

_____

Define Your Purpose

What do you want to show about your topic? Boil the purpose down into one sentence that you can use as a thesis statement.

_____

_____

Identify Your Audience

Write who your audience is and how this affects your writing.

_____

_____

Main Idea and Details *(continued)*

Drafting   To clarify your ideas and organize your essay, fill in the graphic organizer below. Write your thesis statement—the main idea—in the top box. Then list the details that you will use to support your thesis statement. Add detail boxes as needed.

Main Idea

Detail 1

Detail 2

Detail 3

Now use the chart above to help you write the first draft of your essay on a separate sheet of paper.

Main Idea and Details *(continued)*

Revising and Publishing

Revising

The word *revise* means "to see again." When you revise your writing, you step back and look at it with fresh eyes. At this point in the writing process, you think about the big issues. These include the following:

- clarity
- organization
- completeness
- vocabulary

Your teacher can give you a general revising checklist. This will help you learn and practice this step of the process. Remember that this step deals just with big issues. You will deal with details later.

Ask Yourself Questions

To begin revising your main-idea-and-details essay, think about the ideas in your writing. As you reread your work, ask yourself these questions:

- Is my main idea clear?
- Are there enough details to support my main idea?
- Do all the details support the main idea (or do some get off track)?
- Is this pattern a good choice for this topic?
- Do I have an introduction, a body, and a conclusion?
- Do I have smooth transitions to connect ideas?
- Does my conclusion repeat my main idea?

Revising Tip: Take a Break

It can be hard to see the problems in your own writing. For one thing, you may be attached to the words you spent time choosing and arranging. For another, you may be a bit tired of the topic: You just see what you want to see or expect to see. For these reasons it is a good idea to take a break before you start revising. If you have time, set your essay aside for a day. Your eyes and brain will be fresher. You will be better able to think about what needs improvement.

Revising Tip: Read Aloud

As we have said, it is easy to overlook problems in your own writing. One way to find problems is by reading aloud. Your tongue may trip over snags that your eye skips over. If you find yourself stumbling, take a closer look at the passage. Perhaps something does not make sense or is poorly worded. You may also want to tape-record your essay. This lets you hear your words without reading at the same time.

Peer Editing

Another way to improve your writing is to ask for feedback from others. This is called peer editing. In this process, you ask a peer—a classmate, for example—to comment on your essay. Someone who has the same assignment can sometimes help you clarify what you want to say. A peer can also ask you questions that you may not have asked yourself, giving you another angle. Your teacher can give you a peer-editing form to help with this process.

Now revise your first draft. Remember to think about overall questions. You will take care of smaller problems later.

Proofreading

Proofreading is the last stage of the revising process. This is when you take care of grammar, spelling, and punctuation. Your teacher can give you a proofreading checklist to help with this step.

Publishing

Publishing means putting your writing in a form to be shared with others. In school, this may mean neatly handwriting your essay in ink, or printing it out after typing it on a computer. Your teacher will tell you what format and materials are expected.

Now publish your main-idea-and-details essay, following your teacher's directions.

LESSON 8

Opinion and Supporting Evidence

Opinion

An opinion is a belief about something. People may have differing opinions about the same topic. This happens when there are different ways to look at evidence. This also happens when an issue involves emotions.

Evidence

Evidence is proof. Evidence is based on facts, not on feelings or hunches. This does not mean that there is only one possible opinion. There may be conflicting evidence. There may be more than one way to look at the proof.

Model

> Students should wear uniforms to school. Uniforms lessen distractions. This allows more chance for learning. Uniforms also reduce name-calling and bullying. If everyone is dressed the same way, no one can make fun of another student's outfit or style.

> Students should not wear uniforms to school. Middle- and high-school students are creating their identity. Without the chance to express themselves, students will become frustrated. This reduces the chances of their learning.

Both paragraphs above state opinions. Both give thought-out reasons as evidence. Yet they express opposite views.

Fact Versus Opinion

Facts give information that can be checked for truth. It is a fact that a sweater costs X dollars at the mall. It is an opinion that X is too much to spend for that sweater.

Facts are often stated as figures or other proven data. Facts can be checked with reliable sources, such as experts, reference books, and journals. Something is a fact if it is true for many people, not just for one person. Facts do not change with someone's mood.

Opinion and Supporting Evidence *(continued)*

Research Tip:
The Internet   The Internet is a great tool for finding information. One problem, though, is that anybody can write anything on a web page. People can state opinions or rumors as fact. There is no group responsible for checking the truth of statements on the Internet. Be careful when checking facts—look for known experts and organizations.

Try It   Read the following passages. They contain opinions. Some opinions are supported by facts. Others are not. After you have finished reading, answer the questions.

Passage A

The U. S. Navy has a long-standing program of using marine animals in defense missions. The reason is simple. These animals can do some things much better, quicker, and more safely than human divers. Dolphins and sea lions can help protect people and materials.

Scientists have found that these animals have special abilities. Dolphins have sensitive sonar. Sea lions have excellent low-light vision underwater. These traits allow them to easily find mines or divers. The animals swim away safely after tagging a mine or diver. A few of these animals can do the same jobs as many of the human crew members.

The humane treatment of sea lions and dolphins in the Marine Mammal Program is guaranteed by law. The animals are highly trained by professionals. Special veterinarians care for the animals. Independent groups have checked the quality of care the animals receive.

The animals in the program are well-treated and provide a vital service. Protecting the country is what the Navy does. Animals help the Navy do that job. Animals should continue to be used, humanely, to defend the United States.

Passage B

Animals should not be used in dangerous situations just to help people. The use of dolphins and sea lions by the U.S. Navy is barbaric! Using animals—whether for entertainment in a circus, to sniff out victims in a disaster zone, or in combat—is wrong. People who would put an animal in harm's way are not helping the country. They are damaging it!

25

Opinion and Supporting Evidence *(continued)*

Passage C

Animals should not be used in combat areas. It is not the animals' choice to enter dangerous situations to help humans. As shown by the behavior of an escaped dolphin reported in the news, as well as by information from a former military dolphin trainer, dolphins can be distracted from their mission. They do not understand the life-or-death nature of their work. They only do it if they "want" to. This does not give our troops the best protection, which they deserve. For these reasons, the military should stop using animals in its operations.

1. Which passage(s) give evidence for the opinion?

   _____

2. Which passage(s) give emotion as reason for the opinion?

   _____

3. What types of sources does each passage use?

   _____

   _____

4. Which passage is most convincing?

   _____

5. Explain your answer to item 4.

   _____

   _____

   _____

   _____

Opinion and Supporting Evidence *(continued)*

Good Writing Tip: Use Strong Conclusion Words

When you write an opinion essay, you want to convince your readers that you have a good point. You want your readers to agree with you. To do this, you give solid evidence and sound reasoning. You can also use strong conclusion words.

Conclusion Words		
as a result	based on the facts	obviously
as the evidence shows	certainly	plainly
as evidenced by	clearly	surely
as the facts show	for these reasons	therefore

Application

Read the list of writing topics below. Then read the passage. After reading, choose a topic. Write an opinion-and-supporting-evidence essay.

Topics

1. The Iditarod is a worthwhile race. It tests the endurance and courage of people and animals.

2. The Iditarod should be outlawed. It puts both people and dogs in danger.

3. The Iditarod should continue. The dogs get a chance to do what they enjoy.

The Iditarod

The Beginning

The Iditarod, held every March, is an eleven-hundred-mile dogsled race. The course runs from Anchorage to Nome, Alaska. A highly publicized event, the race has both supporters and detractors, or people who are against it. No matter which side you are on, everyone agrees that the race is a difficult test of human and animals against nature.

Some people believe that the race has always existed. This is not so. A man named Joe Redington longed to test himself and his dogs. In 1973, Redington's dream became a reality, and the first Iditarod race was run.

In Alaska, sled dogs were once the only means of transportation. By the 1970s, however, snow–mobiles had largely replaced dogs. There are several reasons for this. *(continued)*

The Iditarod (continued)

Dogs require food, attention, regular exercise, medical attention, and a lot of training. A snowmobile needs gas and oil and the occasional repair—and that's about it.

The goal of the Iditarod was never just speed. A motor-vehicle race would have met that purpose. The goal was to push the limits of human and animals as a team. The Iditarod was created as an adventure, not just a race.

The original plan of the race was to follow a gold-rush mail trail from Knik to Iditarod. Since the town of Iditarod was practically unknown, Redington changed his plan. How about racing through Iditarod on to Nome, a major town? This route followed part of the path followed by the famous diphtheria serum run of 1925. In the serum run, volunteer mushers carried life-saving serum from Nenana, Alaska, to hard-to-reach Nome.

A Long Haul

This change meant the trail was now about eleven hundred miles long—longer than any other sled dog race. The Anchorage Fur Rendezvous World Championship Sled Dog Race was considered a long race at the time of the first Iditarod. That race was only seventy-five miles over three days. The Iditarod usually lasts from nine to twelve days.

Part of the lure of—and argument about—the race is its length. Finishing such a race is truly a test of endurance. On the other hand,

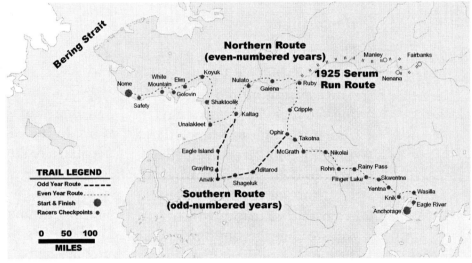

(continued)

The Iditarod (continued)

how wise is such a race? Mushers—the people who drive the sleds—face cold, bad weather, and even dangerous animals on the trail. The dogs work very hard—just to win a race for the musher. The race also promises money for the winner. Again, this is a reward for the musher, not for the dogs.

For the Dogs?

The people involved in the race and the raising of sled dogs say that the dogs love to race. Famous dog drivers such as Libby Riddles, who in 1985, became the first woman to win the race, cite a love of animals and the outdoors as reasons for racing. Dr. Sonny King, a musher and a veterinarian, says that sled dogs love to run and are happiest racing. Breeders point out that the dogs are bred for this activity. It is in their blood.

Race opponents include People for the Ethical Treatment of Animals (PETA). They argue that animals have no choice in the decision to race. Furthermore, PETA points out that about 120 dogs have died over the life of the race. Supporters of the race do not deny that animals are injured and killed during the race. In the early years of the race, some deaths were caused by the inexperience of the mushers. People had not

yet learned that the dogs needed many more calories and plenty of protein and fat to finish the difficult race. Dogs did not always get enough water or rest. In 1974, the second year of the Iditarod, volunteer veterinarians were stationed along the route. Animal medical care and checking has greatly improved. There are now rules to protect the animals. Race veterinarians claim that the current death rate of the race dogs is close to that of regular dogs who do not race. Some organizations still protest the race, including the Humane Society of the United States and PETA. They say that the race veterinarians support the race. The groups argue that any loss is not acceptable.

(continued)

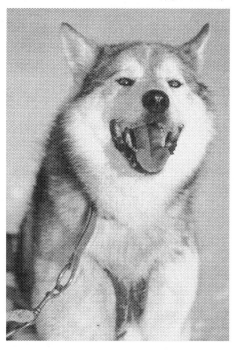

29

The Iditarod (continued)

The Mushers

The Iditarod event is one of the few in which men and women, amateurs and pros, compete against one another. In 1985, Libby Riddles became the first woman to win the race. Another woman, Susan Butcher, won in 1986, 1987, 1988, and 1990. Some races have been won by newcomers to the sport.

Mushing is often a family affair. That is the case for the King sisters, Cali and Tessa. They are daughters of three-time Iditarod winner Jeff King. Cali won the Junior Iditarod in 2002. Her younger sister, Tessa, ran that race in 2003, while Cali moved up to the Iditarod itself. Hannah Moderow, a rising musher, started racing when she was four years old. Her brother has raced the Junior Iditarod four times. Her mother runs sprint dog races. Tyrell Seavey is a third-generation musher.

The Race Is On

Despite protests and money problems, the race goes on. The Iditarod brings money to small Alaskan towns that are sleepy during the rest of the year. The Iditarod has made dogsled racing a recognized sport. It has drawn worldwide attention. One irony of the race is that it was begun as a personal challenge, but now the trail has become so well packed that finishing times are decreasing. There is no need to break trail in snowshoes. There is little chance that teams will become lost searching out trail markers. It is still a difficult race, but in some ways, it has become almost routine.

Opinion and Supporting Evidence *(continued)*

Brainstorming

Brainstorm about the topic you choose. Change the web as needed.

Narrow your Topic

Now analyze your web. Then write your narrowed topic.

_____

Define Your Purpose

What do you want to show about your topic? Boil the purpose down into one sentence that you can use as a thesis statement.

_____

_____

Identify Your Audience

Write who your audience is and how this affects your writing.

_____

_____

Opinion and Supporting Evidence (*continued*)

Drafting   Now that you have completed the prewriting process, you are ready to begin drafting. Use the graphic organizer below to plan and organize your essay. Start by writing your opinion. Then list the evidence that will persuade your readers to agree.

Opinion

Evidence

Evidence

Evidence

Use the graphic organizer above to help you write your first draft on another sheet of paper.

Opinion and Supporting Evidence *(continued)*

Revising and Publishing

Revising

Remember that your first pass at revising deals with big issues: clarity, organization, completeness, and vocabulary.

As you revise this essay, ask yourself questions like these:

- Is my opinion clear?
- Do I give strong evidence and facts to support my opinion?
- Do I rely just on emotion?
- Is this pattern a good choice for this topic?
- Do I have an introduction, a body, and a conclusion?
- Do I use strong conclusion words?
- Is the essay convincing?

You may want to read your essay aloud, or record it and listen to it. This can help you pick up problems by hearing them.

Peer Editing

Asking a peer for feedback can help perfect your essay. Use the peer-editing checklist from your teacher if you are going to ask a peer for comments.

Proofreading

After taking care of the big issues, take care of the details. Check for grammar, spelling, and punctuation errors. Use the proofreading checklist from your teacher to help with this step.

Publishing

When you have revised and proofread your work, make your final copy. Publish your essay according to your teacher's directions.

LESSON 9
Compare and Contrast

Compare Versus Contrast

When you compare subjects, you tell how they are alike. When you contrast subjects, you tell how they are different. In school, you will probably be asked to compare and contrast a variety of things, such as two authors, two books, or two characters in a book.

When you compare and contrast two subjects, you may organize your writing in one of two ways. One way is to explore one subject fully, then cover the same points for your second subject.

Model

Bees are social insects, with most species living in groups. Bees live on pollen and nectar. They make honey to feed their young. They make wax to seal the cells in their honeycombs. These creatures are somewhat furry. They sport the warning colors of yellow and black. As many people have learned the hard way, bees can sting.

Like bees, wasps are social. Unlike bees, they are omnivores. They eat both prey and plants. Wasps collect prey to feed their young. They make their nests from mud or from a mixture of mud and wood pulp. Wasps are generally longer than bees, with narrow waists. Like bees, wasps wear the yellow and black that warns other animals to keep their distance. Wasps can deliver a painful sting, as can bees.

Another way to compare and contrast is to discuss the subjects side by side, point by point.

Model

Both bees and wasps are social insects. Most species live in groups. While bees eat plants and create honey from plant products for their young, wasps capture prey for their offspring. In appearance, bees are furrier and shorter than wasps. Wasps have narrower waists. Both bees and wasps wear the warning colors yellow and black, because both can sting.

34

Compare and Contrast *(continued)*

Good Writing Tip: Use Compare and Contrast Words

Clarity is an important goal in any essay. To help your reader know whether you are comparing or contrasting, you can use signal words. Here are some common words for comparing and contrasting.

Compare Words	Contrast Words
also	although
and	as opposed to
in the same way	but
just as	contrary to
like	despite
likewise	however
on the one hand	in contrast
same	in spite of
similarly	on the other hand
similar to	the opposite of
	unlike
	while
	yet

Try It

Read the following passage. Pay attention to compare and contrast words. When you have finished reading, answer the questions that follow the passage.

Young adult books often feature interesting main characters. Jeffrey "Maniac" Magee from *Maniac Magee* and Stanley Yelnats from *Holes* both turn out to be heroes. Their paths to this status are very different.

Maniac Magee and Stanley Yelnats both have difficult home lives. Maniac, in fact, has no home. He is an orphan who ran away from the miserable household of his aunt and uncle. Stanley, although he has a home and a supportive family, has difficulties, too. His family believes they live under a curse. Stanley's father can never make his inventions work right. And Stanley is convicted of a theft he did not commit.

Maniac is an instant legend—a hero to other characters in the book. Little kids look up to him because of his athletic abilities. The community is amazed by his feats of daring. He inspires an old man to learn to read and convinces some boys to return to school. He is also racially color-blind; he befriends both white and black kids in the racially divided town he winds up in. In the end, he brings the opposing sides together.   *(continued)*

Compare and Contrast *(continued)*

Stanley, on the other hand, is not an impressive character at the start of the book. Unlike Maniac, who tries to change the bad things in his life, Stanley just complains and blames the family curse for them. He is not personable and does not make friends easily. He does not fit in at school or at the reform camp where he is sent as punishment for his crime. As Stanley continues to grow in self-confidence through success at his grueling chore—digging a 5-foot wide and 5-foot deep hole each day in the hard-packed dirt, under a blazing sun—he also grows in character. Like Maniac, Stanley teaches an illiterate person to read. He stands up for a fellow inmate, at great personal risk. In the end, he saves a life.

These two characters, from different backgrounds and with different problems, both accomplish great deeds. They both gain from their own actions. They help others, too. They are both popular heroes to today's young adult readers.

1. List the similarities between Maniac and Stanley.

   _____

   _____

2. List the differences between the two characters.

   _____

   _____

3. List the compare words from the passage.

   _____

   _____

4. List the contrast words from the passage.

   _____

   _____

5. Is the purpose of this essay mainly to show how the characters are alike, or how they are different?

   _____

   _____

Compare and Contrast *(continued)*

Application   Read the list of writing topics below. Then read the passages that follow. After you have finished reading, choose one of the topics. Write a compare-and-contrast essay based on the topic.

Topics

1. Compare and contrast the reasons gods in the myths punish humans.
2. Compare and contrast the punishments of mortals by certain gods.
3. Compare and contrast the personalities of certain gods as shown through their punishments.

Artemis and Actaeon

Artemis, Diana in Latin, was one of the three virgin goddesses of Olympus. She was the goddess of the moon and patron of the hunt. She begged her father, Zeus, to promise never to make her marry. He agreed.

Artemis spent most of her time hunting. One evening she was bathing in her favorite pool in the woods. A young hunter, Actaeon, came by accident to the pool and saw Artemis. She did not wait to find out whether he meant to stare or had just stumbled on her bathing place. Flinging a handful of water in his face, she turned him into a stag.

Soon after, the hunter's own hounds killed him. They did not know their prey was their master. He had no human voice to tell them.

Hera and Callisto

Hera, queen of Olympus and wife of Zeus, was a very jealous goddess. She had reason to be: Zeus often courted other women. In her jealousy, Hera could be cruel and dangerous.

Callisto was one of the mortal women who attracted the attention of Zeus. Hera was furious with her. After Callisto's child, a son, was born, Hera turned her into a bear. Horrified by her new form, Callisto roamed the forest. She kept her human personality and searched out humans, only to run from their dogs. She was frightened of the forest and of other creatures, even though she was now one of the most feared of all. One day, after years of despair, she recognized her grown son. He was a hunter and was about to shoot her with an arrow! Zeus stepped in and saved the bear. He put her and her son in the sky. They are the Great and Little Bear.

(continued)

Compare and Contrast *(continued)*

Hera and Callisto (continued)

Seeing Callisto and her son as constellations angered Hera further. She felt that they were being given a great honor although they had dishonored her. She asked the powers that ruled the oceans not to let the pair sink into the sea like the other stars do. Her request was granted. These two constellations never dip below the ocean line.

Hera and Hercules

Zeus gave his wife, Hera, frequent cause for jealousy. One of his many human mistresses was Alcmena. She became the mother of Hercules. Hera plotted against the boy as soon as he was born.

First, she sent two serpents to kill him in his cradle. Hercules even then was incredibly strong. He easily strangled the snakes.

When Hercules was older, Hera made him insane. In his madness, Hercules killed his wife and children. When he came to his senses, he was full of remorse. As punishment, he agreed to become the slave of Eurystheus, a clever yet cowardly king. Hera helped Eurystheus think of twelve nearly impossible jobs for the hero to do. These became known as the Labors of Hercules.

Midas's Ears

Apollo was the god of music, among other things. Pan was a minor god whose form was half human, half goat. He was also a wonderful musician. The tunes he blew on his reed pipe, however, were no match for the melodies Apollo plucked on his silver lyre.

Midas, a foolish king, was called to be one of the judges in a musical contest between Apollo and Pan. The other judges agreed that Apollo was the winner. Midas wanted to give the award to Pan. In his anger, Apollo changed Midas' ears into those of a donkey.

Compare and Contrast *(continued)*

Prewriting   **Brainstorming**

Brainstorm about the topic you choose. Change the web as needed.

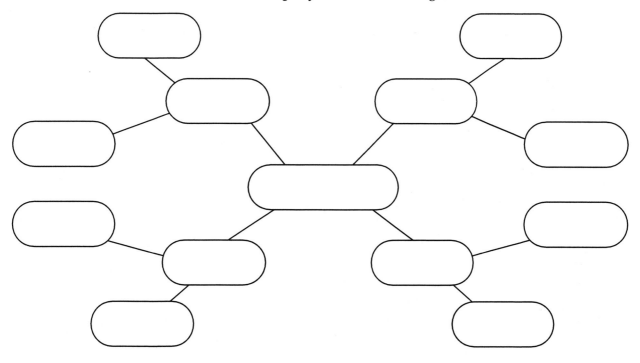

Narrow your Topic

Now analyze your web. Then write your narrowed topic.

_____

Define Your Purpose

What do you want to show about your topic? Boil the purpose down into one sentence that you can use as a thesis statement.

_____

_____

Identify Your Audience

Write who your audience is and how this affects your writing.

_____

_____

 CAWS: Language Arts, 5–6

Compare and Contrast (*continued*)

Drafting   Use the graphic organizer below to help you write the first draft of your compare-and-contrast essay. This graphic organizer is called a Venn diagram.

You may remember the Venn diagram from math class. It is made up of two intersecting ovals. Where the ovals overlap, you write what the two subjects have in common. Where the ovals do not overlap, you write how the subjects are different.

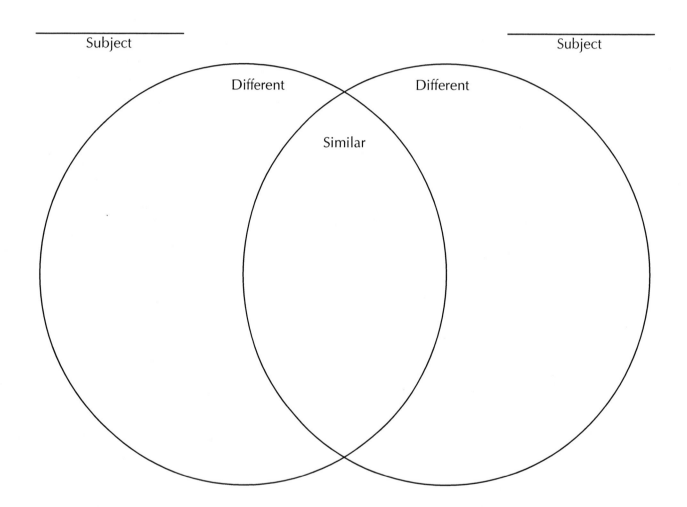

Now write the first draft of your essay on a separate sheet of paper.

Compare and Contrast *(continued)*

Revising and Publishing

Revising

Remember that your first pass at revising deals with big issues: clarity, organization, completeness, and vocabulary.

As you revise this essay, ask yourself questions like these:
- Do I make clear what I am comparing and/or contrasting?
- Do I give enough points of comparison/contrast?
- Is this pattern a good choice for this topic?
- Do I have an introduction, a body, and a conclusion?
- Do I use compare and contrast words?

You may want to read your essay aloud, or record it and listen to it. This can help you pick up problems by hearing them.

Peer Editing

Asking a peer for feedback can help perfect your essay. Use the peer-editing checklist from your teacher if you are going to ask a peer for comments.

Proofreading

After taking care of the big issues, take care of the details. Check for grammar, spelling, and punctuation errors. Use the proofreading checklist from your teacher to help with this step.

Publishing

When you have revised and proofread your work, make your final copy. Publish your essay according to your teacher's directions.

LESSON 10
Cause and Effect

Another common writing pattern is cause and effect. Cause-and-effect essays answer the question "What happened because of *x*?" or "Why did *y* happen?"

Cause

A cause is a reason. A cause may be an event, an idea, or an emotion—anything that is a reason for something else. A cause leads to an effect.

Effect

An effect is a result. It is what happens because of the cause. An effect can only happen if there is a cause.

Order in a Sentence

The cause always *occurs* before the effect. In writing, however, a cause may be *given* after an effect. For example, a classmate might say, "I failed the math test because I didn't study." In this sentence, the effect—the student failed the test—*occurs* after the cause—he did not study. In the sentence, though, the classmate *told* the effect first, followed by the cause. The student could also have said, "Because I didn't study, I failed the test" or "I didn't study, so I failed the test."

Multiple Causes and Effects

There may be more than one cause for a single effect. For example, your classmate might say, "My headache and the noise from the neighbor's party made it impossible to study." Two causes are given for not studying: a headache and noise.

A single cause can have more than one effect. "Because I failed the test, my quarterly grade will go down and I lost TV privileges for a week."

Model

> Hurricane Abel caused a storm surge, or quick rise in water level. This surge tore several small boats from their moorings. Luckily, no one was aboard at the time. Because of the storm warnings, sailors had gone to higher ground inland.

42

Cause and Effect (continued)

The model paragraph gives two chains of causes and effects:

Hurricane Abel → storm surge → tore boats loose

Storm warnings → sailors left → no one aboard damaged boats

In this case, the effect of one cause becomes a cause for the next effect. It is important to keep track of the order of events in a cause-and-effect essay. To help your readers, use words that show the order of events.

Good Writing Tip: Use Signal Words

Some words tell the reader that you are giving cause-and-effect relationships. Using these words helps the reader follow your essay. These words make the relationships between events clear.

Cause-and-Effect Words	
after	led to
as a consequence	since
as a result	so
because	then
caused	therefore
consequently	x led to y
following x, y happened	

Try It

Read the article below. Pay attention to causes and effects. Signal words can help you see these relationships. After you have finished reading, answer the questions that follow.

Dr. Charles Drew

Charles Drew was born in 1904. He did well in school and sports, including football, basketball, baseball, and track. In high school, his performance in these sports led to his receiving the James E. Walker Memorial Medal in his junior and senior years.

After graduating from Amherst College, Drew wanted to attend medical school. He did not have enough money for this, so he went to work for a few years. He became a professor of chemistry and biology at Morgan State College in Maryland.

(continued)

Dr. Charles Drew (continued)

After a few years, Drew could afford medical school. Because he was African-American, however, he had few choices of where to study. Harvard accepted him for the following year, but Drew did not want to wait. He applied to and was accepted at McGill University in Canada.

At McGill, Drew studied under Dr. John Beattie. Beattie was interested in blood transfusions. Blood typing had recently been discovered. Because of this, doctors could avoid the problems caused by giving the wrong blood type to patients. Blood was still very perishable, however. Having the right blood type on hand remained a problem.

In 1930, Drew and Beattie began research on blood storage. Drew graduated from McGill in 1933. He continued his research with Beattie until 1934, when Drew's father died. This event led Drew to move back to Washington, D.C., to take care of his family. In 1935, he started teaching at Howard University Medical School.

In 1938, a two-year Rockefeller Fellowship allowed Drew to continue his research on blood storage. He worked at Columbia University-Presbyterian Hospital in New York. There he studied blood plasma—blood minus the cells—as a substitute for whole blood. Since plasma does not contain the cells that determine blood type, blood-type matching was not necessary. Drew found that separating plasma from blood and refrigerating the two separately made the blood products last longer. They could be mixed together when needed.

Based on his research on blood storage, Drew set up the American Red Cross blood bank. During World War II, he became the medical supervisor of the "Blood for Britain" drive. The need for blood during the Nazi bombings of England was high. Drew began the use of mobile blood banks to treat the wounded.

Dr. Charles Drew died in 1950 in a car accident. He received a blood transfusion, but his injuries were too serious. He is remembered for his discoveries that revolutionized medical science. His work on blood preservation and the creation of blood banks has saved countless other lives.

Cause and Effect *(continued)*

1. What caused Charles Drew to put off medical school?

   _____

2. What effect did blood typing have on medical treatment?

   _____

   _____

3. Why did Charles Drew leave Canada?

   _____

4. What caused Drew's death?

   _____

5. List at least two other cause-and-effect relationships from the article.

   _____

   _____

Application   Read the list of writing topics below. Then read the retelling of "Jack and the Beanstalk" that follows. After you have finished reading, choose one of the topics. Write a cause-and-effect essay.

Topics

1. Why did Jack's mother not tell him about his father? How did the loss of her husband affect the way she raised Jack? Explain.
2. What effect did isolation have on Jack? (How did it affect his dealings with others?) Explain.
3. What motivates Jack to keep going up the beanstalk? What does this say about Jack's ability to control himself? Discuss.
4. Find three examples of Jack making risky decisions. Explain what leads him to make these decisions. Then tell what you think Jack would have done if his upbringing had been different.
5. The man with the beans makes a promise. Does planting the beans have the effect he promised? Explain.

Jack and the Beanstalk

Jack and his mother lived in a small house. There were no other houses nearby, and no other children to play with. Jack did not go to school. Jack never knew his father or how he had died. His mother refused to discuss it when Jack brought it up.

Jack's mother worked hard to provide for herself and her son. She loved her son more than anything and did everything for him. She grew vegetables in a garden that she tended all spring and summer. She harvested the food in the fall and stored enough for the winter. She chopped wood to keep the house warm and to boil water for cooking and laundry. She took care of her cow, which provided milk and cheese in return for hay and water. She gathered nuts and berries in the woods. Occasionally she caught a rabbit or a squirrel in a snare. She saved the meat for Jack because she wanted him to grow strong and stay healthy.

Jack's mother was a quiet woman. Jack loved his mother, but he was idle. She never asked him to help or taught him how to do anything. It did not occur to him to offer to help.

When Jack was about twelve, Jack's mother became ill and could no longer do chores. Finally, she asked Jack for help. She told him to take the hungry cow to town and sell it for money. He was then to take the money and buy food.

Jack had never been to town before; it was a whole day's walk to get there and back. He was nervous but also excited. He had never handled money before. He wondered what it would feel like to hold metal coins in his hand. He had never talked to anyone besides his mother before. How would he ask for what he needed?

After he had walked for a few hours, Jack sat down by a stream to rest. He was dusty and hot. So was the cow. Jack was so tired that he fell asleep. When he woke up, the sun was going down. He would never get to town before nightfall! Jack didn't know what to do.

Just as Jack was about to cry, he heard footsteps approaching. A young man in a brightly colored coat was walking toward him. "Hello, young traveler," said the man. "What are you doing out in the middle of nowhere with a skinny cow?"

Jack readily told his story. "I was on the way to town to sell my cow to buy food. I was so tired that I fell asleep, and now it is too late."

The man said in a smooth voice, "I can see you are in trouble. Maybe I can help. Instead of you

(continued)

Jack and the Beanstalk (continued)

going into town now, why don't I buy the cow from you? Then you will have just yourself to get home."

Jack thought this was a fine idea. The two talked about a price, but the man had no money. "I, too, have been hit by hard times," he said. "But I have something more valuable than gold. Because my own mother once needed help, I'll make a trade with you." He opened a tiny sack that he pulled from his coat pocket. He poured out three green stones. Their color was so bright that they seemed to glow.

Jack was unsure. His mother had said to get money. Still, the stones were very tempting. Surely they must be valuable. "All right. I'll take your three stones for my good old cow."

The man laughed. "They're not stones, my boy. They're beans. Magic beans. Plant them and you will never want for food again." The two made the exchange. The man in the bright coat turned around with the cow and headed back the way he had come. Jack watched until they disappeared into the dark. Then he turned toward home.

It was midnight before Jack reached his house. Before going inside, Jack planted the three beans by moonlight. He watered them and tamped down the earth around them. Then he went inside to bed.

In the morning, his mother woke him early. "I was so worried about you, Jack! What took you so long? Where is the food? I'll make you breakfast."

Jack was excited about his trade. When he told his mother, however, she was not happy. "Oh, Jack! What have you done? Now we will starve!"

Jack did not know what to say. This was the first time his mother had ever raised her voice to him. Confused, he ran outside—and straight into a thick, woody tree trunk. There had been no tree there last night. This must be a beanstalk! He wanted to please his mother, so he started climbing. He planned to pick some beans—surely they would be enormous!—and present her with the food.   *(continued)*

Jack and the Beanstalk (continued)

Jack kept climbing, looking for beans. Eventually he came to the top of the stalk. He looked down. He could barely see the ground below. He looked around. The beanstalk ended on solid ground.

Curious, Jack stepped onto the ground. How odd that there was ground in the sky. Jack wondered what other strange things he might see. He decided to explore.

He followed the path that led from the beanstalk. He came to a large box of a house. Everything about the place was big: oversize windows, tall doorways, a knocker as big as Jack's head. Unable to reach the knocker, he knocked on the bare wood. A tall woman answered the door. "Yes?" she said to the open air. She looked around before looking down. Then she spied Jack.

"Oh! What do you want? Get away before he comes back! Run! Run!" whispered the woman frantically, pushing Jack away. But Jack was not ready to go. He had never seen such a house or such a person, and he wanted to see more. Besides, he was hungry. "Please, may I have a bite to eat? Then I will go and leave you in peace."

The woman was reluctant, but she let him in. She gave him some cheese and bread. "Now hurry, boy. You don't want to meet my husband, the giant. He'll make a snack out of you."

Him? A snack? Jack didn't know what to make of the woman's story. He gobbled his meal and was about to thank the woman when a thunderous boom shook the windows. "Too late!" the woman cried. She grabbed Jack and stuffed him into a cupboard by the stove.

Jack was terrified. He listened as a chair scraped the floor. He listened as a loud masculine voice demanded dinner. He listened as that voice bellowed, "Do I smell fresh meat? Do you have a treat for me, my dear?" Jack didn't like the sound of that.

"No, not tonight. You just smell the leftover beef stew."

(continued)

Jack and the Beanstalk (continued)

The man grunted and began slurping. After his meal, the giant stood up from the table. His wife cleared the table and tidied the kitchen. When the coast was clear, she opened the cupboard. "You wait here," she whispered. "He'll be up for a few more hours. When he goes to bed, I'll open the front door for you. Then run as fast as you can."

After a few minutes, the giant came back to his chair with a goose. "Lay, goose," he commanded. The goose did. The egg in the giant's hand was made of gold! The giant amused himself this way until he had a dozen gold eggs. Then he put the goose down and went to bed.

Jack did not wait for the wife to return. He spotted an open window by the table. He picked up the goose. Holding its beak closed, he leaped up onto the table and out the window. He ran until he reached the beanstalk. He slid the whole way down.

His mother was standing at the bottom. "Oh, Jack! I was afraid I had lost you! I'm sorry I yelled at you. Don't ever run away again!"

"I didn't run away. I just went up the beanstalk to gather beans to eat," said Jack.

His mother tried to hug him, but the goose pecked her. "What is that?" she asked.

"This is a goose that lays golden eggs," answered Jack. "I had never heard of such a thing. But I saw it with my own eyes. We shall never be poor or hungry again!"

Jack's mother sank to the ground and wailed. Jack was confused.

"My boy, you have found your father's goose. He was killed for it, by a greedy giant. Your father befriended him, and in return, the giant ate him!"

"Why did you never tell me this before?" asked Jack. He was not sure how he felt. His mother had never talked about his father.

"Your father was a good man, but too trusting. I didn't want to lose you to the bad people in the world, like I lost him. I didn't want you to search for your father's killer or his goose. So I never told you. Promise me you will never go back up the beanstalk."

(continued)

Cause and Effect *(continued)*

Jack and the Beanstalk **(continued)**

Jack was furious. His father had been kind to the awful giant. And the giant had killed him! Jack could not bear the thought. His rage kept him up all night. His mind raced with ideas for revenge.

The next day Jack's mother took a golden egg to town to buy food and other supplies. While she was gone, Jack went back up the beanstalk. The giant had deprived him of his father; now the giant would pay!

Jack made his way to the giant's house. He climbed up a vine on the wall and peeked in the window. The giant's wife was at work in the kitchen. While her back was turned, Jack climbed in the window and hid himself in the cupboard.

When the giant came home, he sniffed the air. "Ah! Today you found meat! I shall have a feast!" he boomed.

The wife, confused, replied, "I have a chicken pie for your dinner. But no fresh meat." She looked warily around the room.

After dinner, the giant called to his goose. She did not come. Annoyed, the giant instead pulled out two bags of gold and counted the coins until he fell asleep. Jack seized his chance. He slid the heavy bags across the table to the window. He slung one bag over each shoulder and tied them together behind his neck. "Let him see how it feels to be poor," thought Jack as he lowered himself down the vine.

Jack moved as quickly as he could toward his beanstalk. But the bags were heavy and he could only hobble along. The hair on his head stood up straight when he felt a rumbling below his feet. The giant was after him!

Jack scrambled more quickly, but the giant, with his long strides, was soon bearing down on him. Just as Jack reached the beanstalk, the giant reached out and grabbed the bags. They tore in his grasp, sending coins flying. Jack slid down the beanstalk, empty-handed.

(continued)

Cause and Effect *(continued)*

Jack and the Beanstalk (continued)

Again, his mother was waiting. This time she was angry. "Why did you disobey me? The beanstalk is not safe. And you are no better than a thief. Tomorrow I will go to town to buy an axe. I will cut down this trunk myself."

Jack was still enraged at the giant. He was also angry with his mother. While she was in town, he climbed back up the beanstalk.

This time, he knew, the giant would be looking for him. Jack waited until night fell. He again looked in the giant's window. On the table he spotted a golden harp. The giant would not want to lose that! The giant was snoring in his chair nearby. As soon as Jack's outstretched hand touched the harp, the instrument began to scream. Of course, it was a magic harp. "Help! Master!" it screeched. The giant woke up instantly. "Back so soon? I could use a snack!" The giant lunged at Jack but missed. Jack sprinted to the beanstalk and slid down.

Just as he reached the bottom, Jack's mother arrived back from town. "The axe! The axe!" yelled Jack. His mother handed him the tool. Jack chopped furiously at the trunk until the beanstalk toppled. The giant lay in a heap under it, dead.

Jack and his mother moved to town with their goose. Jack learned to tend the garden and studied hard in school. He learned to make friends. He and his mother kept no more secrets.

51

Cause and Effect (*continued*)

Brainstorming

Brainstorm about the topic you choose. Change the web as needed.

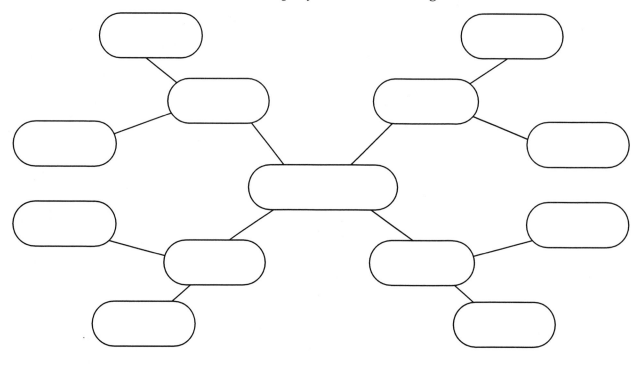

Narrow your Topic

Now analyze your web. Then write your narrowed topic.

_____

Define Your Purpose

What do you want to show about your topic? Boil the purpose down into one sentence that you can use as a thesis statement.

_____

_____

Identify Your Audience

Write who your audience is and how this affects your writing.

_____

_____

Cause and Effect *(continued)*

Drafting   Use one of the following graphic organizers to help keep track of what you want to include in your essay.

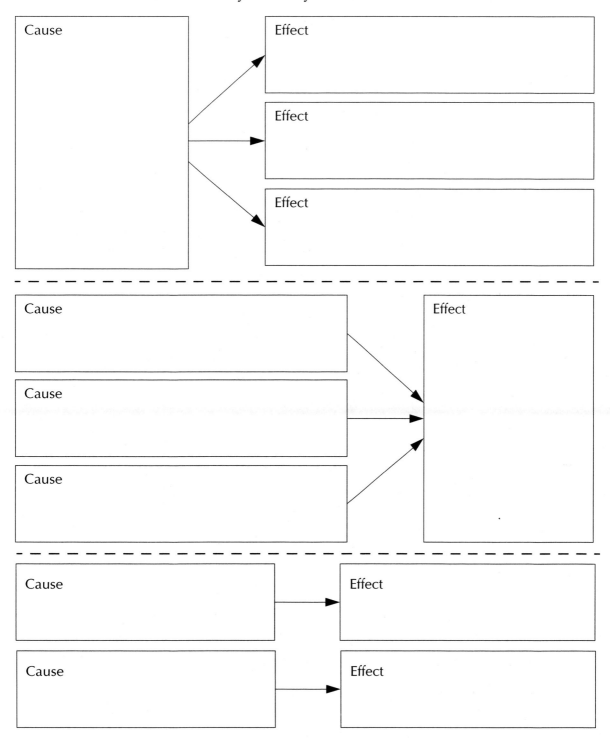

Now write the first draft on a separate sheet of paper.

Revising and Publishing

Revising

Remember that your first pass at revising deals with big issues: clarity, organization, completeness, and vocabulary.

As you revise this essay, ask yourself questions like these:
- Do I show how and why causes lead to effects?
- Is this pattern a good choice for this topic?
- Do I have an introduction, a body, and a conclusion?
- Do I use cause-and-effect words?

You may want to read your essay aloud, or record it and listen to it. This can help you pick up problems by hearing them.

Peer Editing

Asking a peer for feedback can help perfect your essay. Use the peer-editing checklist from your teacher if you ask a peer for comments.

Proofreading

After taking care of the big issues, take care of the details. Check for grammar, spelling, and punctuation errors. Use the proofreading checklist from your teacher to help with this step.

Publishing

When you have revised and proofread your work, make your final copy. Publish your essay according to your teacher's directions.

LESSON 11
Chronological Order

Chrono comes from the Greek word for "time." *Chronological* means "time order." When you put things in chronological order, you list them in the order in which they happen. For example, if you write in a diary or journal, you date each page. This is a chronological record of your thoughts. You can trace how your ideas changed from one day to the next.

Model

> Elena got out of bed at 6:30. She headed to the bathroom and took a shower. After drying off, she quickly brushed her teeth, combed her hair, and got dressed. Next she ate a breakfast of cold cereal and orange juice. Just as the bus pulled up at 7:10, Elena grabbed her backpack and ran out the door.

This paragraph lists Elena's actions in order. The paragraph also tells how the actions are related to each other in time. One way to do this is to list actual times, such as 6:30 and 7:10. If more time passes, you might use words that show the change of seasons or even of years.

You can also use chronological order words. For example, "*After* drying off, she quickly brushed her teeth" tells you that the drying off came first, followed by the brushing of the teeth. Similarly, the word *next* signals a time relationship. The phrase *Just as* in the last sentence tells you that two things—the bus pulling up and the grabbing of the backpack—happened at the same time.

Good Writing Tip: Use Chronological Order Words

Here are some words that signal a chronological order relationship.

Chronological Order Words			
after	during	first, second, third,	later
at the same time	earlier	and so on	meanwhile
before	eventually	followed	next
concurrently	finally	followed by	then
currently		just (as, then)	until

Chronological Order *(continued)*

Try It   Read the following passage. Pay attention to chronological order. After you have finished reading, answer the questions that follow the passage.

> ### History of the Potato Chip
>
> Today, store shelves are packed with bags of potato chips. They come in many varieties: ripples, ridges, salt and vinegar, sour cream and onion, low salt, reduced fat. Potato chips are clearly popular. They did not start out to fill snack shelves, however; they came about because of a snit in a restaurant.
>
> In 1853, a customer at a restaurant in Saratoga Springs, New York, complained. He found the French fries too thick. The chef, George Crum, made a new batch. This time he sliced the potatoes thinner. The customer was still not satisfied. He sent them back a second time. Annoyed, Crum sliced the potatoes paper-thin and fried them until they were crisp and brown. He got a different reaction from the one he expected. The picky customer loved them!
>
> The Saratoga Chips, as they were dubbed, were packaged and sold. The invention of the mechanical potato peeler in the 1920s made it possible to make many chips at a time. Chips then became a common food item.

1. Put the events below in the order in which they *occurred.* (This is not always the order in which they *appear* in a passage!) Number the events from 1 to 5, 1 being the earliest.

   _____ The picky customer loved the thin chips!

   _____ A customer complained that the French fries were too thick.

   _____ Crum sliced the potatoes paper-thin.

   _____ Today, store shelves are packed with bags of potato chips.

   _____ The mechanical potato peeler was invented.

2. List the chronological order signal words used in "History of the Potato Chip."

   _____

   _____

Chronological Order *(continued)*

Application   Read the list of writing topics below. Then read the selection that follows. After you have finished reading, choose one of the topics. Write a chronological-order essay based on that topic.

Topics

1. Mark Twain traveled widely and lived in different parts of the country, including the West. List events—with dates—in Twain's life and work that relate to the West.

2. Show, referring to dates, how the Mississippi River affects Twain's life and work.

Mark Twain's Life and Times

Samuel Clemens was born in Missouri in 1835. He spent his childhood in the town of Hannibal, on the Mississippi River. After his father died in 1847, Clemens became a printer's apprentice. He worked for his brother, Orion, a newspaper publisher in Hannibal. He then spent a year on the East Coast, working in his trade for several newspapers.

Clemens got a break in his writing career when he was hired to write humorous letters about a trip to South America. While traveling down the Mississippi, he took a break to follow a dream. He trained to become a riverboat pilot.

Clemens completed his training and spent three years on the Mississippi. The Civil War began in 1861, and traffic on the Mississippi River was halted. Clemens served for several weeks in the Confederate army. He deserted and joined his brother in the Nevada Territory.

In 1862, Clemens became a writer for the Virginia City *Territorial Enterprise.* He wrote feature stories about daily life in a mining town. It was during this reporting job that Samuel Clemens began signing his work with the pen name Mark Twain. (*Mark twain* was a riverboat phrase meaning "two fathoms [twelve feet] deep.")

Mark Twain moved further west to San Francisco. There he worked for various newspapers and magazines. Twain wrote his famous short story "The Celebrated Jumping Frog of Calaveras County" in 1865. It was based on a story he heard from miners. The story appeared in newspapers across the country.

Twain spent the next several years traveling. Following a trip to Hawaii (or the Sandwich Islands, as they were then

(continued)

Mark Twain's Life and Times (continued)

known), Twain set out on a lecture tour. He commented on the culture he found in Hawaii. In the nineteenth century, lectures were a popular form of adult education. Twain's conversational style and his sense of timing helped make him an excellent public speaker.

Twain took a trip to Europe and the Middle East in 1867. That trip led to a series of articles, gathered in the book *Innocents Abroad*. Published in 1869, it became Twain's first best-seller.

Twain came back to the United States and married Olivia Langdon in 1870. They soon moved to Hartford, Connecticut. Twain put his energies into writing books rather than newspaper articles. He wrote *Roughing It* in 1872, a memoir of his life in the West. *Tom Sawyer* appeared in 1876. *The Adventures of Huckleberry Finn* was published in 1884. These were his two most famous books. They both echo Twain's childhood on the Mississippi. In *Huckleberry Finn*, Huck helps his friend, a fugitive slave, to escape by rafting down the Mississippi.

A publishing company Twain invested in went bankrupt in 1894. To pay off his debts, he went on a worldwide lecture tour. He told of his experiences on that tour in *Following the Equator*, published in 1897. The tour earned Twain more than enough to pay his creditors.

Twain faced personal tragedy when his daughter died in 1896 while he was abroad. His wife died in 1904. Another daughter died in 1909. Mark Twain—Samuel Clemens—died in 1910.

Twain's other books include *The Gilded Age*, written with Charles Dudley Warner and published in 1873. *The Prince and the Pauper*, 1882, was a children's novel. *Life on the Mississippi*, 1883, was a nonfiction book. In 1880, a travel book, *A Tramp Abroad* appeared, and *A Connecticut Yankee in King Arthur's Court* was published in 1889.

Chronological Order *(continued)*

Prewriting   **Brainstorming**

Brainstorm about the topic you choose. Change the web as needed.

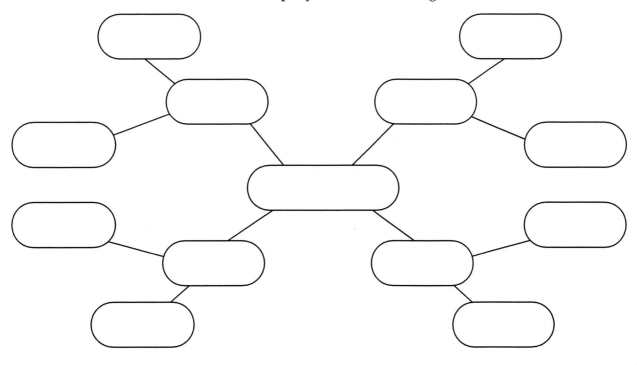

Narrow your Topic

Now analyze your web. Then write your narrowed topic.

_____

Define Your Purpose

What do you want to show about your topic? Write your purpose in a thesis statement.

_____

_____

Identify Your Audience

Write who your audience is and how this affects your writing.

_____

_____

Chronological Order *(continued)*

Drafting   Use the graphic organizer below to write the first draft of your chronological-order essay. Pay particular attention to the order of events.

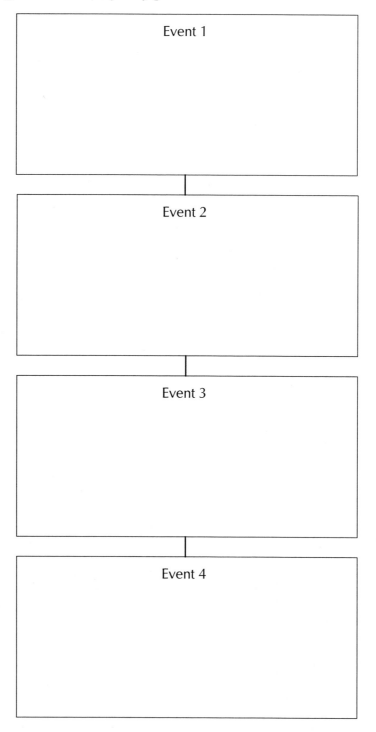

Now write the first draft of your essay.

Chronological Order *(continued)*

Revising and Publishing

Revising

Remember that your first pass at revising deals with big issues: clarity, organization, completeness, and vocabulary.

As you revise this essay, ask yourself questions like these:
- Do I present things in chronological order?
- Is this pattern a good choice for this topic?
- Do I have an introduction, a body, and a conclusion?
- Do I use chronological order words?

You may want to read your essay aloud, or record it and listen to it. This can help you pick up problems by hearing them.

Peer Editing

Asking a peer for feedback can help perfect your essay. Use the peer-editing checklist from your teacher if you ask a peer for comments.

Proofreading

After taking care of the big issues, take care of the details. Check for grammar, spelling, and punctuation errors. Use the proofreading checklist from your teacher to help with this step.

Publishing

When you have revised and proofread your work, make your final copy. Publish your essay following your teacher's directions.

PART 3
Practice Readings

PRACTICE READING A

The Harlem Renaissance

The Great Migration

The word *renaissance* means "rebirth." In the 1500s in Europe, the Renaissance was a time of artistic, literary, and scientific growth. It was the time of change between the Middle Ages and the modern world.

The Harlem Renaissance was also a cultural movement. This one happened in Harlem, New York, in the 1920s and 1930s. One factor in the Harlem Renaissance was the movement of large numbers of African Americans from rural areas in the South to urban centers in the North.

During the years following the Civil War, blacks looked for chances for a better life. Moving to a different place was sometimes part of that search. One wave of African Americans, called "Exodusters," moved West from the South. Fifty thousand moved in 1879, called the year of the "Great Exodus." The Great Migration from 1915–1930 to cities in the North was, therefore, the second such wave. The basic reason for both movements was the same.

With the start of World War I in 1914, companies in the North needed workers. Northern companies began actively seeking black workers from the South. The promise of higher pay, although the cost of living was also higher, was a powerful lure. Cotton was the source of income for many people in the South. The crop had suffered through the 1910s from flooding, pest attacks, and a sharp drop in price.

According to Alain Locke, the respected Howard University professor, the pull of the North was not based just on money. People believed they would have a better life in the North, even though there were still many problems there. These problems included racial violence and poverty. Locke's 1925 publication of *The New Negro* gave a name to the new sense of racial heritage.

The Arts

With the wealth of the 1920s came support for the arts. Through the arts people could express themselves, as individuals and as a group. A vibrant African-American community came together in Harlem. In this community, networks formed among artists in different fields.

(continued)

The Harlem Renaissance (continued)

Jazz, considered the first truly American music, had its roots in Africa. The beat of African music continued in jazz. One trait of jazz is improvisation. This means that much of the music is made up as the musicians play. Sheet music serves as just a general guide. Fats Waller, Louis Armstrong, and Jelly Roll Morton are some of the best-known jazz musicians of the era.

In the early 1920s, jazz became popular in Chicago and then in Harlem. Jazz clubs were common social outlets in the 1920s and 1930s. Scenes of jazz clubs were shown in paintings by Archibald Motley, William Johnson, and others.

Jazz influenced other forms of art. Poet and writer Langston Hughes spent time in clubs, listening to jazz and blues and writing poetry. He tried to write poems that caught the beat of people's lives, the way the music of the time did. He blended the rhythm of jazz into his poems.

Aaron Douglas, called the "Father of Black American Art," used the strong shapes he found in African art in his own work. He illustrated stories, poems, magazines, and books by black writers. One project was a series of paintings for James Weldon Johnson's 1927 book of poetry, *God's Trombones: Seven Negro Sermons in Verse.*

Lois Mailou Jones's well-known painting *Les Fetiches* was created in 1938. This painting shows several African tribal masks. Jones was one of the first female painters to use African imagery in her work. Sculptor Richmond Barthe did something that had never been done before. He created busts of African-American subjects in stone and bronze.

During the Harlem Renaissance, African-American literature, music, and art gained some acceptance in mainstream American society. Black artists no longer had to hide their racial identity. Indeed, it was a time to express personal identity by examining daily concerns, including race.

Exotic Pets

Domesticated animals are animals that have been raised by humans for a long time. Such animals may be very different from the original wild animals they came from. Animals with certain traits—traits attractive to humans—have been bred to create more animals with those traits.

Exotic means "excitingly different or unusual." Exotic pets are animals that have not been raised by humans for a long time. They are, basically, wild animals. No matter how cute they are, wild animals have wild instincts. Of course, all domesticated pets were once wild animals. It is only over time that a type of animal becomes domesticated.

Exotic pets have become more popular in recent years. According to the Animal Protection Institute, several groups oppose keeping certain exotic pets. These groups include the American Veterinary Medical Association (AVMA), the United States Department of Agriculture (USDA), and the Centers for Disease Control and Prevention (CDC).

The exotic nature of exotic pets makes them attractive. Owning a unique pet can be a status symbol. It can be very interesting, since it is not a common experience. Having an unusual pet gives people a chance to learn about and share knowledge of their special animal.

Both those who support and those who oppose keeping exotic pets agree on some points. Exotic animals require exotic care. Not all veterinarians are trained to provide medical care for unusual pets. Nor are all owners able to provide the sometimes expensive food and living space exotic pets need.

Exotic pets can be a danger to humans and the environment. In 2003, a monkeypox outbreak was caused by infected prairie dogs. These animals had been sold as pets. Many reptiles carry and spread salmonella, a bacteria that causes illness in people. Wild animals also tend to bite. Putting exotic pets back into the wild can endanger native animals. It can also affect the balance of the ecosystem. That is what

(continued)

Exotic Pets (continued)

happened with starlings and house sparrows. They were released in New York in the nineteenth century. These birds now live all over North America. They compete with native birds and destroy crops.

Webster's Collegiate Dictionary defines a pet as an animal that is kept for pleasure rather than for utility, or work. Maybe the definition of "pet" depends on what gives the owner pleasure. If you want a friendly, cuddly pet, you probably do not want an exotic pet. They are, by nature, not used to living with humans. If you want to watch an unusual animal and are willing to care for it, you may be interested in an exotic pet.

Secret Codes

Secret codes have been used by many cultures since ancient times. Children like to invent secret codes using letters and numbers. Special pens can be bought for secret writing. The ink is invisible when it dries, but can be seen when rubbed with another pen. Spy movies show people using secret passwords. Cryptography—writing in secret codes—is used to send information while keeping it hidden from certain people.

Written Codes

Cryptography has been used in America since the nation's beginning. Invisible ink was used by spies on both sides of the Revolutionary War. A person would write a normal letter in regular ink. Between these lines, the person would write the secret message in invisible ink. The reader treated the letter with either heat or a chemical to reveal the hidden words.

Another way to encode a message was to refer to a book. Both the sender and the receiver must have the same book. The sender found the needed word in the book. Then he or she noted the page number and where on the page to find the word. This could be done by counting lines and words and writing them in a specific order. The receiver had to know the method for finding the words. With the book in hand, the receiver could then find the words and write out the message.

Code Talkers

Native Americans were called on during World War II to encode secret messages. In 1942, Philip Johnston thought of a code based on the Navajo language. Johnston was the son of a missionary to a Navajo reservation. He had learned the Navajo language as a child. The language was useful as a secret code because it had no written symbols and was spoken only by the Navajo. The language lacked words for some terms such as *submarine* and *airplane*. New words were added to stand for these terms. The language and the additions were made into a code.

Thirty Navajo code talkers were recruited. They learned the code and gave messages flawlessly. The Japanese never broke the Navajo code.

(continued)

Secret Codes (continued)

Cryptography is used on many levels. You may have a signal that tells a friend to save you from a boring conversation. Security companies and clients decide on secret passwords that mean that everything is—or is not—all right if an alarm goes off. Parents and their children often have private codes of their own. The drive in humans to communicate information is strong; so is the drive to keep information secret.

Songs and Quilts

During the time of slavery in the United States, a network called the Underground Railroad worked to help runaway slaves to freedom. Some negro spirituals—songs sung by slaves—held secret information. "The Gospel Train" and "Swing Low, Sweet Chariot," for example, contained information about the network.

Quilts were another covert, or hidden, way to send messages. Symbols were sewn into the quilts. To most people, the quilt would be just a quilt. To someone who knew the symbols, the quilt could serve as a map to a stop on the Underground Railroad.

CAWS: Language Arts, 5–6

PART 4
Graphic Organizers

BRAINSTORMING WEB

Use this chart to brainstorm writing ideas. Add or subtract circles as needed.

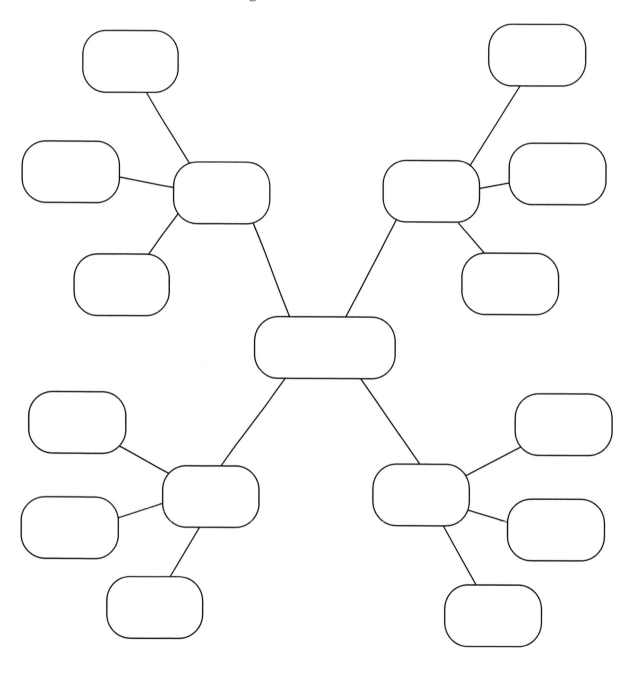

Main Idea and Details Chart

Use this chart to organize your main idea and the details that support it. Add or subtract boxes as needed.

Main Idea

Detail 1

Detail 2

Detail 3

OPINION AND SUPPORTING EVIDENCE CHART

Use this chart to organize your opinions and the evidence that supports them. Add or remove boxes as needed.

Opinion

Evidence

Evidence

Evidence

COMPARE AND CONTRAST (VENN) DIAGRAM

Use this diagram to show how two things are similar and different.

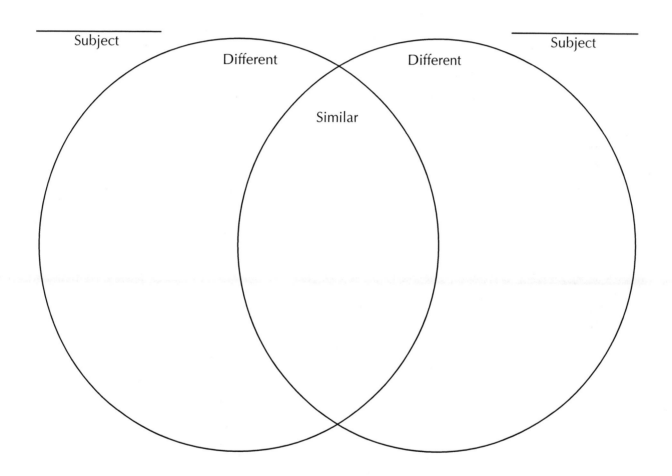

CAUSE AND EFFECT CHART

Use this chart to show the relationships between causes and effects. Add or subtract boxes as needed.

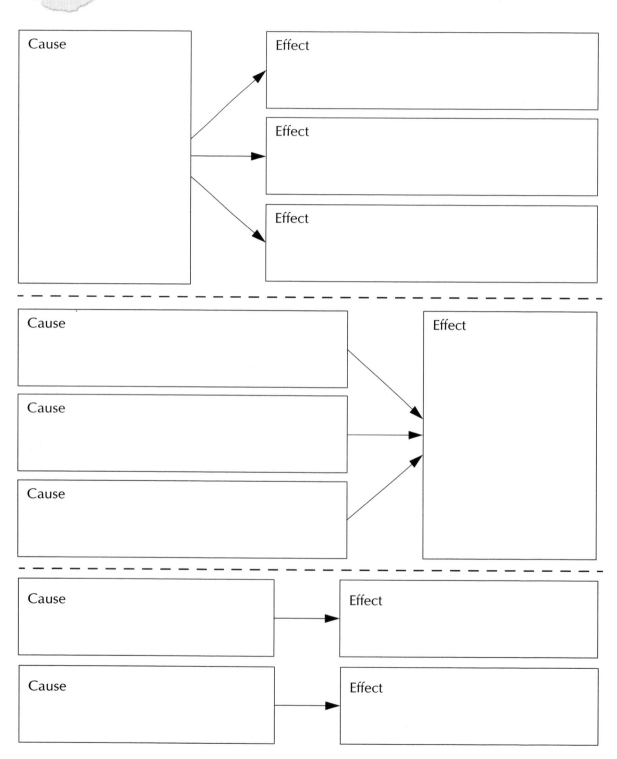

CHRONOLOGICAL ORDER CHART

Use this chart to organize events in the order they happened. Add or subtract boxes as needed.

Event 1

Event 2

Event 3

Event 4

REVISING CHECKLIST

The revising step is the time to look back at your writing and handle the big issues, including organization, clarity, completeness, and word choice. Use the checklist below to help you revise your written work. You may want to add some particular problem areas to the bottom of the list.

Organization	Yes	No
Did I use a logical pattern or organization?		
Did I follow my pattern consistently?		
Clarity		
Did I use signal words to clarify my pattern or organization?		
Did I make my purpose clear?		
Did I write a clear thesis statement?		
Did I include any unnecessary sentences?		
Completeness		
Did I include an introduction, a body, and a conclusion?		
Did I include enough information to support my thesis statement?		
Word Choice		
Did I use specific words rather than general words?		
Did I use vocabulary appropriate for my audience?		
Other things to check for:		

PROOFREADING CHECKLIST

Use the following checklist to polish your written piece before you publish it.

Grammar	Yes	No
Did I write any run-on sentences?		
Did I leave any sentence fragments?		
Do all my sentences make sense?		
Do my subjects and verbs agree?		
Did I use the correct verb tenses?		
Mechanics		
Did I capitalize correctly?		
Did I use commas, periods, semicolons, and colons correctly?		
Did I use apostrophes, question marks, quotation marks, and exclamation points correctly?		
Did I spell everything correctly?		

PEER-EDITING FORM

Use this form to offer feedback to a classmate—and to receive feedback on your writing.

Some guidelines:

- **Start with praise.** Talk about the best, most interesting, most exciting, most insightful, or most whatever part of the piece.
- **Show respect.** As a writer yourself, you know how hard it can be to put your thoughts on paper—you would not want your efforts to be treated lightly.
- **Stick to the point.** Address what you have been asked to address.
- **Be specific.** Saying "This section wasn't clear" is too broad and not very helpful. Something like, "Could you explain more about X? I think I'd understand better how Y happened then." gives the writer a better idea of the problem and a solution.
- **Ask questions.** Revisions are up to the writer. If you phrase your suggestions as questions ("Can you tell me more about Z here?" rather than "Tell me more about Z."), a writer can respond and then choose to incorporate that change or not.

Writer: _____

Title: _____

Area(s) to be discussed: _____

_____

Good points: _____

_____

_____

_____

Questions: _____

_____

_____

_____

_____

_____

PART 5

Teacher's Guide

Part 1: Prewriting

Lesson 1: Writing Process Review

This brief lesson reviews the writing process. If students are not familiar with the writing process, this lesson serves as an introduction to the concept and the steps involved. Extra modeling may be helpful for students for whom the writing process is new.

Answers will vary.

Lesson 2: Brainstorming

You may want to emphasize that brainstorming is fun—students can write whatever comes to mind without concern for form. Brainstorming is also a personal process; it is up to the writer to decide what is kept or discarded from a brainstorming session.

Remind students that they should not try to "fill in" every circle of the web provided; it is just a guide. Adding or ignoring circles shows that students are really letting their ideas flow!

Try It

Webs will vary.

Lesson 3: Narrowing Your Topic

Narrowing a topic may be less burdensome if students realize that it makes their job of writing much easier later in the process. This is the time to think about what is the most interesting—or the easiest, or the quickest—topic to write about.

A completed brainstorming web is a useful tool in narrowing the topic. Students can see what they know and what they might need to find out.

Try It

Narrowed topics will vary.

Lesson 4: Purpose

This lesson clarifies students' role in defining an assignment. Even if they are given a topic, they must put it into their own words.

Try It

Thesis statements will vary.

Lesson 5: Audience

Students may have never really thought about their audience; they may never have written for anyone besides a teacher. They will not always be writing for school, though, and it is useful to bring the audience into students' consciousness. Even in school, teachers other than you may grade a paper, and some tests students may take will be graded by complete strangers. Considering the audience is a good habit.

The Effects of an Audience

Answers will vary.

Think About Your Audience

1. Answers will vary, but students might suggest using literary vocabulary. Contest entrants might also tailor their subject matter to what they think the judges would like or expect to hear.

2. Answers will vary, but students might suggest using shorter sentences, shorter paragraphs, and simpler vocabulary.

3. E-mails will vary.

Part 2: Writing Strategies

This section introduces graphic organizers that will help students organize their writing. In earlier lessons, students practiced using one graphic organizer, the brainstorming web. Specific patterns common in language arts writing are modeled and applied: main idea and details, opinion and supporting evidence, compare and contrast, cause and effect, and chronological order.

Lesson 6: Drafting

Common Patterns in Language Arts

Answers will vary.

Lesson 7: Main Idea and Details

Try It

Items 2 and 10 are main ideas. The rest are details.

Application

Webs, organizers, and essays will vary.

Lesson 8: Opinion and Supporting Evidence

Try It

1. A and C

2. B

3. A: scientific experts, independent groups; B: only personal emotion; C: news reports, expert

4. Answers will vary, but students will likely choose A or C.

5. Answers will vary but should include that factual evidence is used.

Application

Webs, organizers, and essays will vary.

Lesson 9: Compare and Contrast

Try It

1. They are both heroes, both have difficult home lives, both teach someone to read, both accomplish great deeds.

2. Maniac is likable, makes friends easily, is admired. Stanley is not personable, does not make friends easily, complains rather than acts, and does not fit in.

3. both, both, like, both

4. although, on the other hand, unlike, different

5. The passage shows how the boys are alike despite their differences.

Application

Webs, organizers, and essays will vary.

Lesson 10: Cause and Effect

Try It

1. He did not have enough money.

2. Doctors could avoid the medical complications of nonmatching blood types.

3. His father died, so Drew moved to Washington to take care of his family.

4. He died from injuries in a car crash.

5. sports performance led to medal; being African-American led to few choices of

schools; unwillingness to wait led to applying to and attending McGill; because plasma does not contain cells, no type matching is needed

Application

Webs, organizers, and essays will vary.

Lesson 11: Chronological Order

Try It

1. The correct chronological order is 3, 1, 2, 5, 4.

2. Today; In 1853; this time; a second time; until; in the 1920s; then

Application

Webs, organizers, and essays will vary.

Part 3: Practice Readings

This section contains readings that students may draw on while writing essays. All these readings may be supplemented by student research and personal experience. Possible writing topics are listed below, but students may generate others.

Practice Reading A: The Harlem Renaissance

1. Explain events that led to the Harlem Renaissance.

2. Explain some effects of the Harlem Renaissance.

3. Support this main idea with details: The Harlem Renaissance led to collaboration among artists.

Practice Reading B: Exotic Pets

1. Answer this question: Should people keep (or be allowed to keep) exotic pets? Support your opinion.

2. Compare and contrast mainstream pets and exotic pets. Include personal experience as well as other evidence.

3. Explain reasons people decide to keep exotic pets.

4. Explain the effects of people owning exotic pets.

Practice Reading C: Secret Codes

1. Explain the reasons people and groups use cryptography (secret codes).
2. Trace the uses of cryptography throughout U. S. history.
3. Explain the effect of the Navajo code.

Part 4: Graphic Organizers

The organizers in this section may be copied for students to use. The revising, proofreading, and peer-editing organizers should be distributed when students reach those steps.

Assessment Rubric

The assessment rubric on page 85 may be modified to use with any assignment. It may be helpful to share the rubric with students before they begin their assignment so that they know what to expect in the grading process. This rubric is only one possible tool for assessing written work; conferences, students own self-assessments, and portfolios can also contribute to a student's grade.

Assessment Rubric

Criteria	Points				Score
	1	**2**	**3**	**4**	
Organization	Sequence of information is difficult to follow.	Some information poorly placed.	Information presented in reasonable order that reader can follow.	Information presented in logical, interesting order that reader can easily follow.	___
Content Knowledge	Insufficient grasp of information; work does not communicate adequate information.	Writer demonstrates basic understanding of concepts.	Writer is at ease with content.	Writer demonstrates full knowledge of concepts and elaborates.	___
Audience	Writer has not used appropriate tone and/or vocabulary and has not considered audience's knowledge.	Writer has used some appropriate vocabulary and has attempted to address audience's knowledge.	Writer has used appropriate tone and vocabulary and has accurately assessed audience's knowledge.	Writer has used appropriate tone and vocabulary, has accurately assessed audience's knowledge, and has engaged audience with thought-provoking ideas.	___
Completeness	Not enough information; thesis statement not sufficiently supported; no or weak conclusion.	Adequate information; thesis statement supported; weak conclusion.	Sufficient information; thesis statement supported; strong conclusion.	Sufficient information; thesis statement well supported; strong conclusion.	___
Grammar and Mechanics	Piece has four or more grammatical/spelling/usage/punctuation errors.	Piece has three grammatical/spelling/usage/punctuation errors.	Piece has no more than two grammatical/spelling/usage/punctuation errors.	Piece is free of grammatical/spelling/usage/punctuation errors.	___
Other:		.			___
Comments				Total:	___

Share Your Bright Ideas with Us!

We want to hear from you! Your valuable comments and suggestions will help us meet your current and future classroom needs.

Your name_____Date_____

School name_____

School address_____

City _____State _____Zip_____Phone number (_____)_____

Grade level taught_____Subject area(s) taught_____Average class size_____

Where did you purchase this publication?_____

Was your salesperson knowledgeable about this product?　　Yes_____　　No_____

What monies were used to purchase this product?

____School supplemental budget　　____Federal/state funding　　____Personal

Please "grade" this Walch publication according to the following criteria:

	A	B	C	D	F
Quality of service you received when purchasing	A	B	C	D	F
Ease of use	A	B	C	D	F
Quality of content	A	B	C	D	F
Page layout	A	B	C	D	F
Organization of material	A	B	C	D	F
Suitability for grade level	A	B	C	D	F
Instructional value	A	B	C	D	F

COMMENTS:_____

_____

What specific supplemental materials would help you meet your current—or future—instructional needs?

_____

Have you used other Walch publications? If so, which ones?_____

May we use your comments in upcoming communications?　　____Yes　　____No

Please **FAX** this completed form to **207-772-3105**, or mail it to:

Product Development, J. Weston Walch, Publisher, P. O. Box 658, Portland, ME 04104-0658

We will send you a **FREE GIFT** as our way of thanking you for your feedback.　**THANK YOU!**